TULSA CITY-COUNTY LIBRARY

HRJC

D0936432

JUN 2007

SandCastle™

Math Made Fun

Skip Count by 10, Let's Do It Again!

Tracy Kompelien

Consulting Editors, Diane Craig, M.A./Reading Specialist
and Susan Kosel, M.A. Education

ABDO
Publishing Company

Published by ABDO Publishing Company, 4940 Viking Drive, Edina, Minnesota 55435.

Copyright © 2007 by Abdo Consulting Group, Inc. International copyrights reserved in all countries.
No part of this book may be reproduced in any form without written permission from the publisher.
SandCastle™ is a trademark and logo of ABDO Publishing Company.

Printed in the United States.

Credits
Edited by: Pam Price
Curriculum Coordinator: Nancy Tuminelly
Cover and Interior Design and Production: Mighty Media
Photo Credits: ShutterStock, Wewerka Photography

Library of Congress Cataloging-in-Publication Data

Kompelien, Tracy, 1975-
    Skip count by 10, let's do it again! / Tracy Kompelien.
      p. cm. -- (Math made fun)
    ISBN 10 1-59928-541-X (hardcover)
    ISBN 10 1-59928-542-8 (paperback)

    ISBN 13 978-1-59928-541-2 (hardcover)
    ISBN 13 978-1-59928-542-9 (paperback)
    1. Multiplication--Juvenile literature. 2. Counting--Juvenile literature. I. Title. II. Title: Skip count by
ten, let's do it again. III. Series.

QA115.K665 2007
513.2'13--dc22
                                                                          2006017372

SandCastle Level: Transitional

SandCastle™ books are created by a professional team of educators, reading specialists, and content developers around
five essential components—phonemic awareness, phonics, vocabulary, text comprehension, and fluency—to assist young
readers as they develop reading skills and strategies and increase their general knowledge. All books are written,
reviewed, and leveled for guided reading, early reading intervention, and Accelerated Reader® programs for use in
shared, guided, and independent reading and writing activities to support a balanced approach to literacy instruction.
The SandCastle™ series has four levels that correspond to early literacy development. The levels help teachers and
parents select appropriate books for young readers.

Emerging Readers	**Beginning Readers**	**Transitional Readers**	**Fluent Readers**
(no flags)	(1 flag)	(2 flags)	(3 flags)

These levels are meant only as a guide. All levels are subject to change.

J 513.2 K836st 2007
Kompelien, Tracy, 1975-
Skip count by 10, let's do it

To skip count by 10

is to count in groups of 10.

Words used
when skip counting:
group
same
tens

My  have 10 toes.

My have 10 fingers.

This is a group of

10 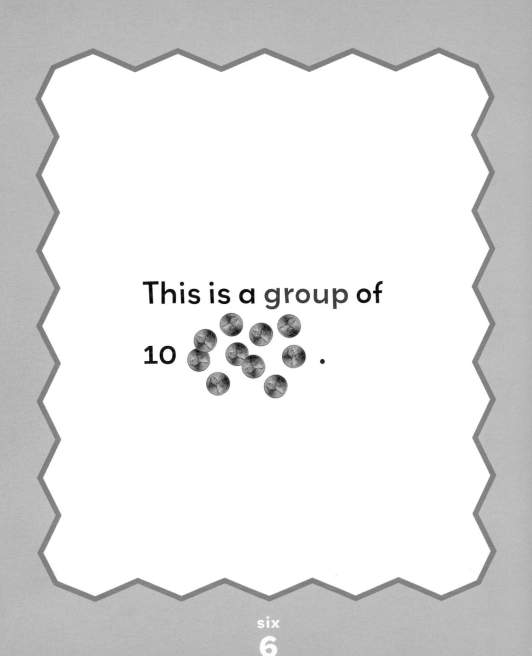 .

10 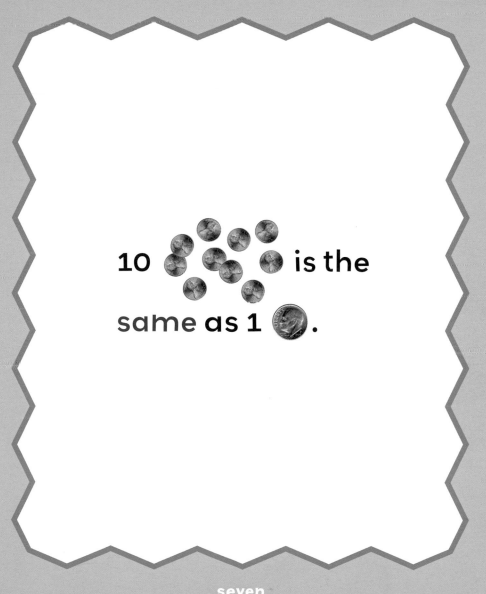 is the same as 1 .

I group 10

together.

These and these are equal groups.

Skip Count by 10, Let's Do It Again!

10 peppermints
are on the plate.
Ted adds 10 more
at a fast rate.

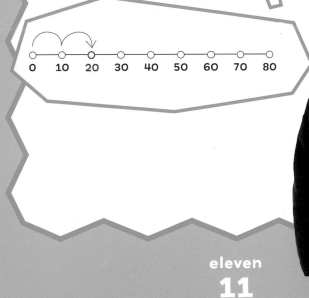

twelve
12

Next Ted adds 10
more to the group.
"That makes 30,"
he says with a whoop!

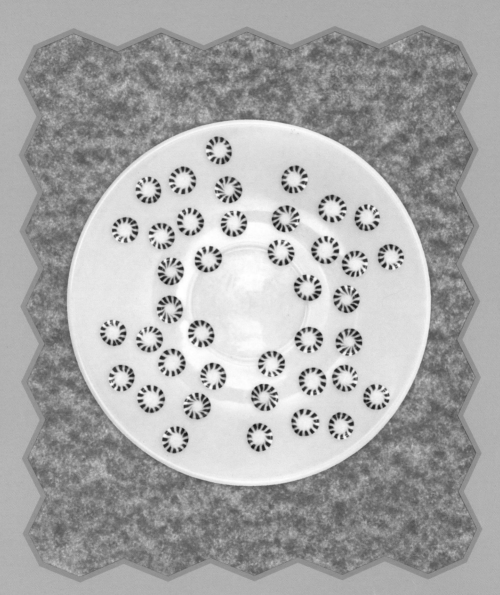

fourteen
14

Ted decides the more peppermints the better. He adds 10 more and skip counts like before.

0 10 20 30 40 50 60 70 80

Skip Count
by 10
Every Day!

When I count my dimes,
I skip count by tens.

1 dime equals
10 cents.

eighteen
18

When I share candy with my sister, I skip count the pieces by tens until the candy is divided equally.

Counting by tens is a good way to count big numbers.

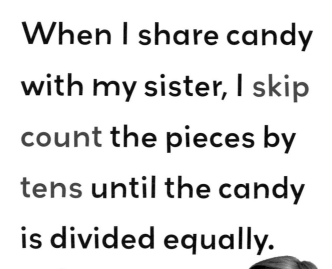

When I bake cookies,
I put 10 on each sheet.
I can skip count by tens
to figure out the total
number of cookies.

twenty-two

22

Can you skip count to find how many leaves there are?

Start by dividing the leaves into groups of 10!

Glossary

dime – a coin that is worth 10 cents.

divide – to separate into equal groups or parts.

equal – having exactly the same amount. Equal groups have the same amount in each group.

piece – a part of a whole.

rate – a degree of speed. The term *fast rate* means that something is done in a very short amount of time.

whoop – a loud, happy shout.